To my Son Ashley.

Without you, this book would not be possible.

You opened up my eyes to a bigger world around me. You opened up my heart more and taught me how to be more patient, forgiving and understanding.

Copyright © 2022 Leanne Batty. All rights reserved.
Cover and illustrations by Zoe Saunders.

No part of this publication may be reproduced in whole or in part, or stored in a retrieval system, or transmitted by any means, electronic, mechanical, photocopying recording or otherwise, without written permission of the author.

Paperback ISBN: 978-1-7397607-0-0
Hardcover ISBN: 978-1-7397607-1-7
Ebook ISBN: 978-1-7397607-2-4

All rights reserved.
Published by Leanne Batty.

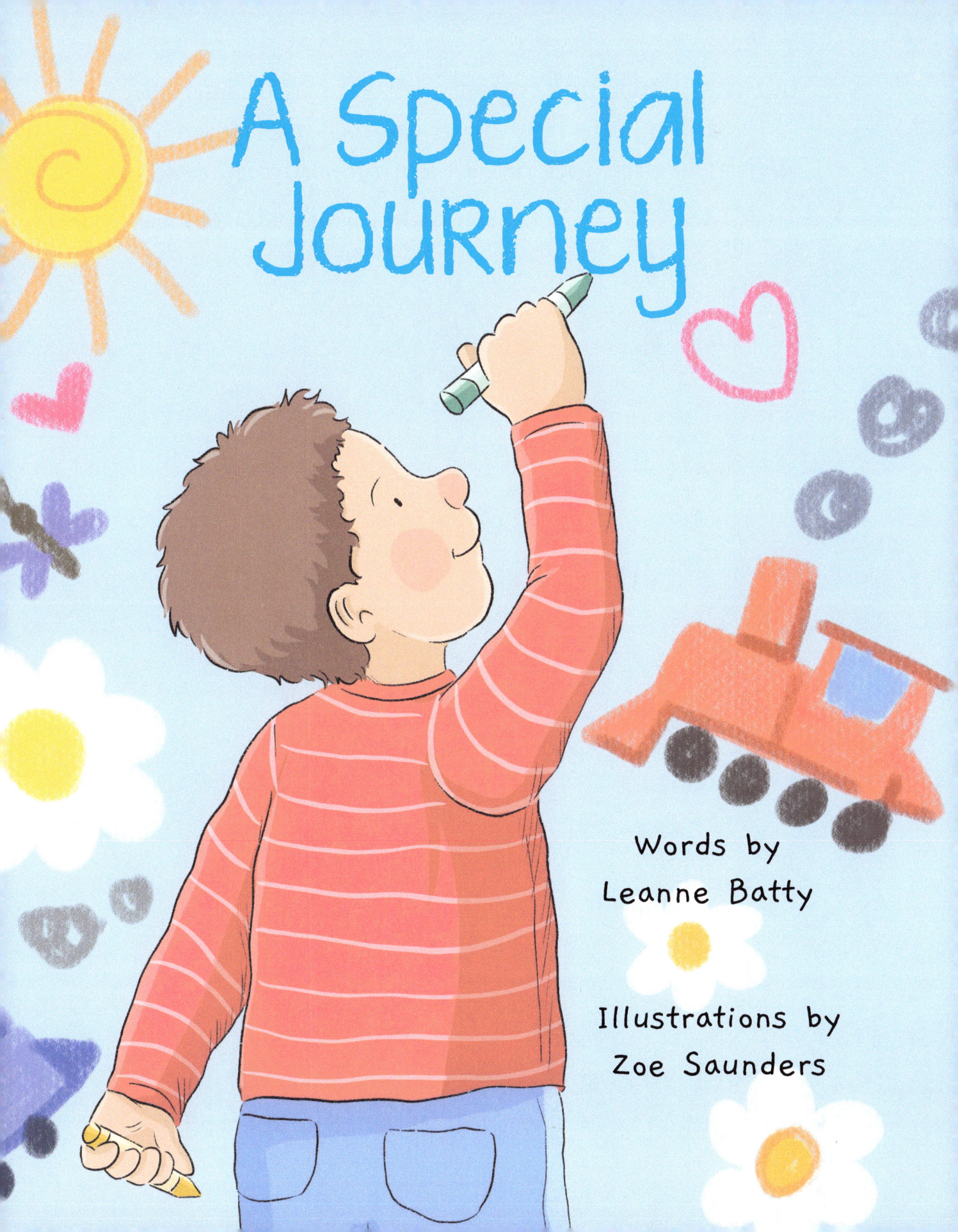

Let me introduce myself. My name is Ashley.
I am a little boy on a special journey.
What is that journey? I know you may ask.
I must complete a particularly important task.

For I was born with Autism and ADHD,
I would like to teach you all what it is like to be me.

My hair is short and brown,
my eyes are big and blue.
I have ten fingers and toes,
just like you do too.

I smile when
I am happy.

And I cry
when I am sad.

I sometimes like you,
can get angry or mad.

Mum tells me it is called emotions
and that we all have the same.

I struggle to express them.
But it may get better with my age.

When I was smaller,
it would take me a while to speak.

But with help, love and encouragement,
my sentences got better every week.

Now that I am growing, I can over talk too much.

Often interrupting conversations
reaching out for my mum's hand to touch.

There are times I tend to fidget
and roll around on the floor.

Or I can sit quietly, listen to music and draw.

I make unexpected actions,
like clapping, stimming or a finger click.
The doctor told me, it's ok Ashley.
For they are what we call a 'tic'.

I liked to play with trains
and put them in a colour coordinated line.

I must have a routine, each and every time.

I am incredibly good with numbers.
My brain works in ways that others cannot see.

But I am not so good at riding a bike.
I often fall and graze my knee.

My food can be quite repetitive.
My favourite is pizza, nuggets or chips.
But they must be plain textured mind,
with no extra tasty side dips.

I can often walk into a road,
unaware of the hazards coming my way.
Mum pulls me closely into her and tells me,
"Don't worry my dear, everything will be ok."

I have no sense of danger
and would often sneak outside.
A game of hide-and-seek I thought,
I know just the place to hide.

My family always encourage me
to remember the special boy that I am.

"You can do anything you set your heart to sweetie."
Yes, yes, I can.

I have an important task to do
to help you all to see,
that it is perfectly perfect to be you,
him, her or me.

For every child is different, so special
and unique in their own way.
For many, Autism and ADHD live inside of us
every day.

I am starting to get older now.
I am 11 to be precise.
I am beginning to start a new chapter
on this special journey called life.

I will continue to be me
and do all the amazing things I enjoy.
For there will come a day
when I am no longer a young boy.

I promise that you are special and loved
more than you could know.
Your mum, dad, family or carer,
will always tell you so.

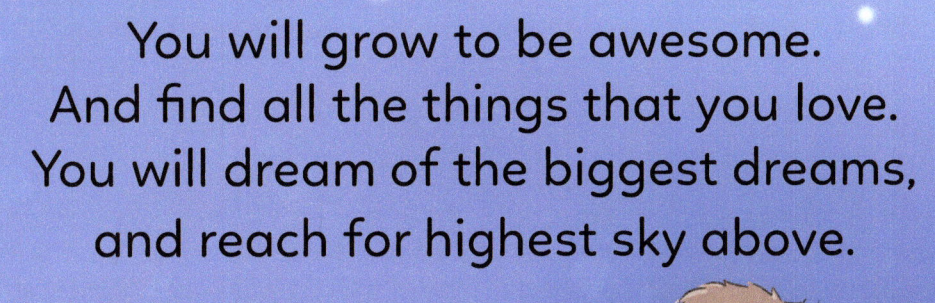

You will grow to be awesome.
And find all the things that you love.
You will dream of the biggest dreams,
and reach for highest sky above.

Please always remember
to be brave, courageous and kind,
to everyone you meet
on life's special journey.

But especially to your mind.

Frequently asked questions

What is Autism?

First of all, Autism is not an illness or a disease. Autism is a life long developmental condition affecting 1 in 100 people in the UK alone. You cannot catch Autism. It is something you're born with or first appears when you are very young. You do not grow out of Autism. If you're Autistic, you're Autistic your whole life.

Autism impacts on the way a person communicates and how they experience the world around them. Autism is described as a spectrum condition. This means that while autistic people, including Asperger's syndrome, share certain characteristics, they will be highly individual in their needs and preferences.

How do I know if my child has Autism?

Signs of Autistic traits can vary enormously. If you feel that your child is showing Autistic traits then your first point of call would be to speak to your GP who can do a referral for your child to a pediatrician and follow out an assessment? I have listed most of the traits that my son had that were noticed and picked up by myself and his nursery school teacher, which was later confirmed by our GP that an assessment was needed.

- Repetitive behaviors.
- Lack of interest (for children) in playing with other children.
- Lack of understanding of facial expressions or tones of voice.
- Lack of emotion for others, or over emotional.
- Literal understanding of words : a person with Autism may have difficulty in understanding common metaphors such as 'it's raining cats and dogs.'
- Special interests which may be or become obsessive.
- Avoiding eye contact.

- Becoming upset and distressed by certain sounds, taste or smell.
- Non-verbal, delayed speech.
- Repetitive movements such as flapping their hands, rocking back and forth. This is also known as "stimming."
- Find it hard to make friends or prefer to be on their own.
- Struggle with how to put their thoughts and feelings into words.

Please note that each individual will have their own level of needs. This is only a small guideline and some of the common traits of Autism.

How is Autism diagnosed?

Autsim cannot be diagnosed by a simple blood test or examination. Instead, Autism and Adhd is diagnosed by using observation and looking at the individual's development history. If you feel like your child may be on the spectrum then my list of advice would be as follows:
- Write down a list of all the signs that you feel your child has relating to Autism.
- Monitor these signs and make a diary of any behaviors.
- Speak to your child's Nursery, or school setting. Explain your concerns. And ask them to monitor too. If your child is struggling when ask to speak to the schools SENCO (Special Educational Needs Coordinator).

What causes Autism or Adhd?

There is no one cause of Autism or ADHD. Research suggests that Autism develops from a combination of genetic and non-genetic or environmental influences. There is strong evidence to suggest that Autism can be caused by a variety of psysical factors, all of which affect the brains development. It is not due to emotional deprivation nor is it because of child's vaccines. Evidence suggests that both Autism and ADHD may be genetic. Scientists have been atempting to identify which genes might be implicated. But it is likely that multiple genes are responsible, rather than a single gene.

Help and Support

Autism

National autistic society
www.autism.org.uk

Ambitious about Autism
www.ambitiousaboutautism.org.uk

Autism speaks
www.autismspeaks.org

NHS
www.nhs.uk

Sendiass

ADHD (Attention Deficit Hyperactivity Disorder)

adhdfoundation.org.uk

www.mind.org.uk

www.adhdcare.co.uk

chadd.org

Anxiety/Mental health for children

www.kooth.com

CAMHS

www.youngminds.org.uk

childline 0800 1111

Samaritans 116 123

About the Author

Leanne lives in Cheshire with her son Ashley, dog Molly and cat Binx.

She attended University to study a degree in Criminology and Law. However, due to her desire to help others, she switched careers in 2020. Leanne now works with children who have special educational needs at her local school.

Leanne has a passion for reading. Her goal is to be able to educate others about neurodevelopment disorders. She continues to do this by sharing her own experiences of being a mother to a child with special educational needs.

Leanne's son received a diagnosis of Autism, ADHD and Sensory Processing Disorder in 2018. Since then she has taken the time to educate herself and those around them to ensure that Ashley is given the best support possible, and to try to understand the world through Ashley's eyes.

www.ingramcontent.com/pod-product-compliance
Lightning Source LLC
Chambersburg PA
CBHW042255100526
44589CB00002B/28